Maximizing Cash Flow - The Path to Prosperity

This book is designed to provide competent and reliable information regarding the subject matter covered, based on the specific experiences and knowledge of the author. The reader acknowledges that the author and publisher are not engaged in providing legal, financial, or other professional advice, and this book is not a substitute for the advice of an attorney, financial or tax advisor, or other professionals. Every person and organization is different, and laws and business practices vary from state to state and country to country. If legal or other assistance is required, the services of a professional should be engaged by the reader. The author and publisher specifically disclaim responsibility for any liability incurred from the use of the contents of this book.

ISBN: 978-0-578-98393-6

All photographs are courtesy of the author.

This book is dedicated to the
most important people in my life:

My Wife, Judi Alberton

My Son, Bill Share

My Son and Daughter-in-Law,
Dave and Gwen Share

My Grandchildren,
Layton and Willow Share

Thank you for your
Unconditional Love and Support!

TABLE OF CONTENTS

FOREWORD

This book is for entrepreneurs and wantrapreneurs at the beginning of their journey, those struggling to survive and grow, successful business owners who are always looking to improve on what they've created, and professionals working in large organizations with a passion to make good things happen (I call them Intrapreneurs). Regardless of your company's level of success, ***change happens,*** and you must be prepared to adapt quickly. Major disruptions can and will occur unexpectedly, including growing too fast. How you respond will impact your chances for success. My focus in writing this book is to give you the tools necessary to succeed by Maximizing Cash Flow!

First, thank you to my son, Bill Share (www.billsharedesign.com), the branding and graphic design expert for my company as well as for this book. Bill created the cover page, the graphics, formatting, editing, proofreading, as well as providing constant support, including joint development of my website at www.sharebusinessgrowth.com. Bill, your work, creativity, professionalism, and passion are outstanding and precise, and your efforts to bring this book to life have been invaluable. Thank you also to Tina R. Phillips for your thorough editing from a business perspective. Your involvement is truly appreciated.

Thank you to Margaret Somer, Northeast Region Director (retired) of the Small Business Development Center at Salem State University, for your help in defining my business, hiring me to teach seminars for the SBDC Northeast Region, mentoring, and for supporting not just my company, but also those of my clients who I had sign up for SBDC advisory assistance. Margaret, you have been an inspiration to me as I continue to grow my business.

Thank you to Alan Adams, my long-time friend, colleague, mentor, college accounting, finance, and entrepreneurship instructor, textbook author, and collaborator on several of my real-life projects. Alan was a highly successful entrepreneur, small business consultant, and is now a professor of Finance and Entrepreneurship at Dean College in Massachusetts. You have invited me to speak to many of your classes over the years, interviewed me on Dean College radio, and have been instrumental in my development as a Cash Flow Solutionist™. Alan, you have been a truly important part of my professional and personal life, which I greatly appreciate.

Thank you to the innumerable colleagues, co-workers, clients, and friends - too numerous to name here - who, over the past decades, have impacted my personal life and professional career in positive ways. Thank you to all the attendees of my seminars, classes, and presentations over the past years, from pre-teens to college students to retirees to small business owners to professional service providers. Thank you to the numerous bankers, venture capitalists, angel investors, and other financing professionals for your insights, suggestions, and support of my clients' requirements. Every one of you, with your questions, comments, interactions with others, after-seminar discussions, and post-meeting follow up, have made me a better presenter, and improved my product and service knowledge to benefit my clients.

Most importantly, thank you to my wife, Judi Alberton, for your love and unwavering support of everything I do, personally and professionally. This book, and my incredibly happy life, would not have happened without you. You are the world to me!

INTRODUCTION

You are smart, innovative, creative, and open to meeting all challenges, both expected and unexpected, and will adapt to any and all changes.

You are passionate about your company, motivated to make it succeed, and will continuously build a team of key people who believe in your dream and will join you in making the company successful.

You are humble enough to know that there are always new business ideas and management concepts to learn from other people and experiences. You accept constructive criticism as a positive, and you learn from past mistakes.

Entrepreneurs and business owners, for the most part, are experts with their products or services, but even the best may fall short on knowing how to build and manage the business around them. You must be proactive in developing and implementing the best opportunities for growth. The difference between being "***proactive***" versus "***reactive***" may be the difference between success and failure.

This book was specifically written to help businesses succeed by Maximizing Cash Flow. This has been my passion during my 22 years in the large corporate world, and since 1993, working with entrepreneurs and business owners, helping them build their dreams. In my career, both domestically and internationally, I have been involved with virtually everything many owners and managers may not even imagine as being critical to growing and managing a business. In addition to decades of working with start-ups through successful companies, and having spent most of my career teaching on a variety of subjects, I am bringing my knowledge, experience, and real-life stories together to provide this book to help your business succeed.

This book is divided into two sections:

- ***The Big Picture*** section contains my foundational elements of starting, building, and growing a business, including definitions, and descriptions of the key processes necessary for you to build your successful business. It describes a variety of situations and reasons "Why" you should perform certain tasks. To me, "Why" is as important as all the "How to" books, which show you how to develop your company or write a Business Plan, but do not provide why the information and steps are necessary to implementing the Business Plan and managing your company to success.

- The ***Your Action Steps*** section details what I believe is the most critical concept in managing a business: Maximizing Cash Flow. This section includes **specific action steps** you and your team should and must perform within your own company. Maintaining and growing cash on hand and consistent recurring revenues will enable you to do everything necessary to grow your business, such as hiring key staff, purchasing equipment, expanding facilities, and meeting all expense and financial/tax obligations. Your decisions will generate the growth and momentum you are pursuing - if you do it right!

To be successful, business owners must focus their attention on the key requirements presented in this book.

"Every decision you make, every action step you take, impacts your Cash Flow."

Why Do Small Businesses Fail?

My experience shows that 10 out of 10 small business owners want positive Cash Flow, and the more cash and liquidity they have, the better. When you have all the cash required to reach and surpass your goals, you are positioned for success. If you do not have sufficient cash, you will likely struggle.

Yet, there are numerous studies on why small businesses fail. A recent 2020 study[1] shows small business failure rates of:

First Year: 21.5% Second Year: 30.0%

Fifth Year: 50.0% Tenth Year: 70.0%

Approximately 75% of these failures are caused by:

- Lack of sufficient Working Capital and recurring Cash Flow
- Entering an industry with little or no industry experience
- Hiring an inexperienced team which doesn't work well together
- Failing to recognize the market has no need for their products or services
- Ignoring what customers want
- Not being flexible; not adapting to changing trends

Based on my own experiences, I would also include:

- Poor pricing and understanding of product and service costs
- Lack of passion by the management team
- Failure to acquire and implement the necessary systems and operating processes

[1]2019 Small Business Failure Rate: Startup Statistics by Industry, 2020, Joseph Camberato, www.NationalBusinessCapital.com"

Why Do Small Businesses Succeed?

Businesses succeed when all the stakeholders - management team, employees, bankers, investors, attorneys, external accountants and auditors - work together to implement the Business Plan and continue managing to it on an ongoing basis.

In my decades of experience, I find that successful businesses have a number of basic characteristics in common. These include:

- They have a well-thought-out vision for the organization and have identified the steps necessary to implement that vision over a reasonable period of time. This is having an excellent Business Plan with solid financials, projections, and budgets.

- They are well capitalized and have sufficient cash to meet their objectives.

- The management team and employees have a passion for the business to succeed, which means they will "get things done right" for achieving their business mission. They know how to get more from less.

- They invest in the right systems. A solid Business Plan achieves nothing if you don't invest in the processes and systems necessary to achieve success. I've seen good business opportunities fail because the owners did not provide the necessary infrastructures, systems, and processes, even though they had the financial resources to do so.

"The more prepared you are to meet any challenges, the more effective your decision-making, the better your chances for success!"

THE BIG PICTURE

THE BIG PICTURE

CHAPTER 1

IMPORTANT PROCESSES AND DEFINITIONS

It is necessary to begin your path to prosperity by understanding key definitions of Cash Flow processes, which are presented throughout this book, along with case studies from real-life situations for illustrative context. Remember, there are no guarantees to success or failure, but properly positioning your company provides the best path to success.

BUSINESS PLAN

- ***Develop a Comprehensive Business Plan.*** Your Business Plan is first and foremost the operating manual of your company. It provides the goals and objectives of your business, including the strategies and financial measurements to help your business achieve success.

- ***Effectuating the Business Plan.*** An effective Business Plan is one in which the company succeeds. Therefore, you won't know whether or not your Business Plan is effective until the company is progressing and growing as expected. A solid and effective Business Plan must be well executed to achieve success. It must be well-researched, clearly presented, and requires the full support of your stakeholders - management, employees, bankers and/or investors, attorneys, accountants, and others. It requires a forecast of at least three years of solid, supportable financial projections, with Year One being your first-year Budget.

- ***Managing the Company to the Business Plan.*** This is essential to the process. As noted above, your Business Plan is first and foremost the operating manual for your company. Follow the steps described in detail in each section, and you will quickly identify and rectify obstacles that arise unexpectedly or create and initiate new opportunities.

- ***Monitoring and Modifying.*** When monitoring your company's performance, you will invariably hit obstacles or new opportunities, which you must swiftly identify and implement action steps. If you've prepared your Business Plan thoroughly and have been monitoring performance continuously, your decisions will be much more effective. Your Business Plan is a living document and must change as circumstances and business needs dictate.

~ *A TRULY GREAT BUSINESS PLAN STORY* ~

A number of years ago, a colleague of mine decided he wanted to start his own breakfast/lunch café in a New England state, and he was going to do it right. He quit his high-paying job, approached the owner of a similar style restaurant, and asked if he could work in the restaurant for free for six months, performing every role from dishwasher, to cook, to server. This would give him the knowledge and experience he would need to make his new venture successful.

During this time frame, he wrote his Business Plan, and it was solid. When he completed his six-month experience, he set out to identify the proper location for the café. He discovered the perfect space in a good location, where another restaurant

had gone out of business. He called the landlord and made an appointment to meet with him.

When they met and spoke about the restaurant space, my colleague handed the man his Business Plan and asked him to read it. They met again a couple days later. He asked the landlord about the Business Plan and got back a very strong, positive reaction. At that moment, my colleague suggested that if he were to lease the location to him for zero cost, the landlord, who owned the location, would be compensated with equity in the new restaurant. The landlord agreed and they made the deal.

The café opened a short time after, and it was immediately profitable, beginning in its first month in operation. This was truly a win-win for both parties. It also is a great example of how out-of-the-box thinking can help finance a new company.

CASH FLOW

My simple definition of **"Cash Flow"** is to have more cash coming into your company than cash going out in any specific time frame. However, what is most important for you and your company is to develop consistent, recurring revenues to provide enough cash on hand to meet your current and future needs. When you reach this goal, the path to growing your company becomes far easier. You are Maximizing Cash Flow.

CASH CRUNCH

I define **"Cash Crunch"** as having insufficient Cash Flow to sustain your business going forward. It may be ***"negative"*** in which your expenses are greater than incoming revenues. In this scenario, you are draining your cash reserves, requiring you to make important future decisions on where and when to spend the funds you ***do*** have, and which payments for operating expenses, purchases, new hires, and other expenses must be delayed.

It may be ***"positive"*** in which cash is coming into your company at a faster rate than going out, but not at a high-enough level to meet all of your objectives. For example: You are generating positive Cash Flow of $5,000 per month, but you require at least $100,000 to purchase an important piece of equipment or hire a key employee. With insufficient funds or cash reserves, you will likely have to delay purchasing that item or hiring that key employee, with an unfavorable impact on your company. Possibly you may have to access a bank line of credit, or add more owners' equity, but these options can be expensive.

~ *CONVENIENCE VERSUS PROFITABILITY* ~

I was writing a Business Plan for a food service start-up, and was watching "Restaurant Impossible" on the Food Network for insights. One show had a restaurant which would run out of specific food products, and the owner would run next door to buy the needed products at a convenience store. The increased cost of doing this drastically impacted the restaurant's food costs and severely hurt profitability. The host also mentioned how much time the owner spent outside the restaurant while running to the convenience store. It was several hours a month that she was away, during the busy dinner time. Keep in mind: actions like this add up, and decisions based on panic rarely succeed.

"Maximizing Cash Flow is Essential to Success!"

I sometimes describe managing Cash Flow akin to someone having a medical problem. At first, you don't feel well and don't know why, so you take over-the-counter medications in hopes that the symptoms will go away. They don't and, instead, they continue to worsen. At some point, you will be in such pain that you have to go to a doctor to cure you. However, the doctor cannot make a diagnosis or offer any possible remedies without understanding the underlying causes of your problems. A series of tests is necessary to identify the cause of the pain.

This exact concept occurs when your company is experiencing pain, which may include growing pains, and you don't know the cause. Trying to internally self-diagnose your company's problems using existing staff will likely have a negative impact. Taking current staff away from their own jobs to identify problems and develop solutions will cost you significant funds, including lost opportunity costs. It may be Cash Flow beneficial to outsource your specific issues to an external expert, who will likely be able to identify the causes of the problems and offer specific remedies more quickly, while allowing your staff to focus on growing the business.

FINANCIAL STATEMENTS

Reference to financial statements mentioned throughout this book cover the following:

- A ***Chart of Accounts*** is a critical component of your financial reporting system. It is, in effect, a complete listing of every account included in your company's trial balance, including assets, liabilities, stockholders' equity, revenues and expenses, that are utilized to generate all the financial statements on which you manage your company's performance. You and your accountant must create a Chart of Accounts based on the reporting requirements for your company. Virtually all automated bookkeeping systems (e.g., QuickBooks) provide the capability to set up your complete accounting system, including transactions, and all your key financial schedules. Be sure you implement the Budget module in the system for future analysis purposes.

- A ***Profit and Loss Statement,*** also known as an Income Statement, is a financial report that shows all revenues and expenses, which result in either a net profit or loss for the company, over a specific period of time. Most automated bookkeeping systems allow you to show this report in summary form, or in detailed account form. This report provides you with the data necessary to determine where problems may exist. A Profit and Loss Statement includes non-cash transactions such as depreciation.

- A ***Balance Sheet*** is a snapshot view of a company's financial position at a specific point in time, such as end of month, end of quarter, or end of year. The Balance Sheet is divided into three sections: Assets, Liabilities, and Stockholders' Equity (note that Assets = Liabilities + Stockholders' Equity). Assets reflect the probable future economic benefit of the company's resources, Liabilities represent claims against the company by creditors, and Stockholders' Equity reflects the net profit or loss from the Income Statement, referred to as Retained Earnings, as well as the capital contributions and financing provided by the company's owners.

- A ***Cash Flow Statement*** is a report which strictly shows the company's inflows and outflows of cash transactions; therefore, it differs from the Profit and Loss Statement, which may contain sales on credit or expenses not yet paid, as well as other non-cash transactions. It is the Cash Flow Statement that most professionals examine to determine the financial viability of a company. Without cash, a company cannot pay its bills, and will likely not survive. In many cases, a company may show it is profitable via the Profit and Loss Statement, but the Cash Flow Statement shows the company cannot survive.

BUDGETS

- ***Budgets*** are preliminary projections for managing the financial performance of a company. It is essentially a quantified statement of projected revenues and expenses by account, that should be consistent with the Chart of Accounts listing. Budgets should be compared against actual financial statement results of a company on a frequent basis to determine if and where financial adjustments may be required.

The most effective presentation of financial statements is showing Actual results versus Budget for the same period of time. It provides sufficient detail to more quickly identify potential issues or problems and develop solutions. I suggest providing these statements to your stakeholders on at least a monthly basis for discussion and to determine if any action steps are required, or as support for obtaining financing.

~ PROFIT AND LOSS ACTUAL VERSUS BUDGET REALLY WORKS ~

At one point in my career, I was the Senior Financial and Administrative Manager of the Worldwide Financial Services Department at Bank of Boston Corporation. This Department included the International Private Banking Division (IPB), with over $1 Billion in Assets Under Management and several hundred million dollars in Deposits Taken from foreign nationals, and Deposits Placed with financial institutions. IPB had at that time three overseas and five domestically incorporated business units.

Every month, I reviewed all of the financial statements for each of the business units within the Worldwide Financial Services Department, as well as each specific unit's reports. During my review of IPB's Profit and Loss Actual versus Budget schedule, I noticed one overseas subsidiary with an interest rate margin on Deposits Taken (deposits received from foreign nationals) much lower than its budgeted interest rate margin, and much lower than the other seven units. I immediately created an Excel spreadsheet to monitor the interest rate spreads for each of the eight units to focus in on any problem. I also discussed my discovery with the IPB Division Executive and the head of the Worldwide Financial Services Department.

This process of comparing Actual versus Budget identified one overseas unit that was the outlier. I called and spoke with the controller of that unit and within an hour, she discovered that the IPB officers were using an outdated rate sheet when quoting interest rates to clients.

Working with IPB management and the controllers of each of the eight units, we developed and implemented a new division-wide policy and procedure to correct this problem permanently. This entire process was completed within a matter of days. When the next quarter's Profit and Loss Statement was distributed, the interest rate margin increased by 25 basis points (one quarter of a percent) on a $250 million balance. That was money that went directly to the bottom line, proof positive that reviewing Actual versus Budget financial statements is critical to success.

BOARD OF DIRECTORS/BOARD OF ADVISORS

Every company should have either a Board of Directors or a Board of Advisors, comprised of individuals whom you trust to provide input into the success of the company. I recommend a small company meet with their Boards at least monthly. There are important distinctions between the two Boards:

- The ***Board of Directors*** oversees the performance of the company and, importantly, each member has a legal and fiduciary responsibility to act in its best interests. The Board of Directors is a group of elected individuals who typically are not involved in the day-to-day operations for larger companies, but may be much more directly involved in smaller companies. It is not unusual for members of the Board of Directors to also be equity owners in smaller companies, where they have a more direct role in moving the business forward. In my experience, the best members of a Board of Directors are those who together provide a broad background and experience in marketing and sales, finance, technology, legal, as well as industry expertise. Depending on the company size and whether it is a public or private company, a Board of Directors may or may not be required. For example, the smallest companies do not necessarily require a Board of Directors.

- The ***Board of Advisors*** provides similar characteristics as the Board of Directors, but this Board does not have any legal or fiduciary responsibilities to the company. This Board's members may be professionals, friends, or others with broad backgrounds needed by the business, and periodically meet with the management team to discuss the company's progress or issues and offer ideas and possible connections. Members of a Board of Advisors typically do not have equity ownership, nor are they involved with the day-to-day operations.

~ *SUPPORT FROM UNEXPECTED SOURCES* ~

I spent 10 years in the International Banking Group at Bank of Boston Corporation. At that time, it was the nation's 17th largest bank holding company, with assets of over $65 Billion, and had the fourth largest international branch network in the country. International Banking's top executive announced that we would hold the first International Banking Group employee outing at a local country club on a specific day in July when the weather would be warm. Staff at all levels - from administrative assistants and clerical workers to executives - were invited, including a significant number of officers from subsidiaries and branches around the country and the world. Activities included golf, softball, tennis, various outdoor games, use of the resort's swimming pool, as well as all

activities available at the club. Over 125 employees gathered together to enjoy the entire day, and celebrate with a clambake in the evening.

The day arrived and the International Banking Group took over the country club. Many people bonded with others, which enhanced the relationships, and new ones developed as well.

At the clambake, the food was great, the conversations non-stop, and a number of awards were given out - some serious and some hilarious. What really happened is that so many people formed bonds that when we all went back to work the next day, the mindset of International Banking had changed noticeably for the better. In a few cases, new ideas or concepts were raised and discussed to improve upon existing projects. The positive impact on how the International Banking Group functioned after this event cannot be understated.

The big picture here is that everyone is involved in growing the company. I was introduced to two administrative assistants, each of whom had a college degree in business. When hiring opportunities arose, I succeeded in hiring both of them as financial analysts, where they excelled. Sometimes a fun, business-social event will benefit your company immeasurably, as well as provide possible incentives for key employees to stay with the company. Even better, I still maintain contact with some of my International Banking colleagues some 30 years later.

THE BIG PICTURE

CHAPTER 2

WHY PREPARE A BUSINESS PLAN?

As previously mentioned, my personal experience shows that 10 out of 10 small business owners want positive Cash Flow, and the more cash they have, the better. When you have sufficient cash required to reach and surpass your goals, you are positioned for success. If you do not have sufficient cash, you will likely struggle. I use the word "positioned" throughout this book to remind everyone that there are no guarantees of success or failure.

"The Business Owner is responsible for positioning the Company for Success or Failure!"

My five-decade involvement in a variety of business environments with companies both large and small, showed me that an effective Business Plan is the most important document in your company. It is the only document that reconciles and links every aspect of your business, and it is critical that all your stakeholders - management team, key employees, staff, lenders and investors, attorneys, accountants, insurance agents - adhere to the Business Plan. This process will not work well if the owner goes through it alone, it is kept on a shelf and never used, or if the key stakeholders do not agree with the strategies and data presented. Before going any further, you first must understand WHY you need a Business Plan.

I define an effective Business Plan as one in which the Company grows and prospers based on managing to it. This means it must be implemented in order to achieve success. Otherwise, it is just an irrelevant document taking up space on a shelf. It will not help your company succeed.

I suggest there are seven primary purposes for a Business Plan:

Purpose 1: The Business Plan is the Operating Manual for the Company. When properly prepared, the Business Plan provides a detailed checklist of all steps necessary for each aspect of the company, both qualitative and quantitative. By managing to the Business Plan, the management team will be positioned to quickly identify the source of problems or opportunities, then develop and implement effective remedies.

Purpose 2: Links all aspects of a Company. The Business Plan is the only document which links every aspect of a company's functions. The quantitative financial projections must flow from the qualitative descriptions, and there must not be any disconnects. For example, you will likely hit obstacles if your sales staff sells 50,000 widgets per month, but the manufacturing component has a capacity of producing only 10,000 widgets per month. ***PROOFREADING*** is essential. I once reviewed a Business Plan, in which the owners projected $6,000,000 in annual revenues. However, the financials reflected $50,000 for twelve months, or $600,000. Luckily this mistake was caught before the owners presented the Business Plan to investors.

Purpose 3: Identifies Strengths, Weaknesses, Opportunities, and Threats (SWOT) and how you will address each component. A key tool in preparing an effective Business Plan is to perform a SWOT Analysis. This analysis details what management believes are its Strengths and Weaknesses from an internal perspective, and the Opportunities and Threats it faces from an external perspective. For each Strength, Weakness, Opportunity, and Threat identified, the Business Plan should describe how the Company will address each line item. The key is to identify how you will support and build on your strengths, take advantage of your opportunities, minimize weaknesses, and protect your assets against threats. This is an ongoing process. How best to understand and prepare a SWOT Analysis is described in Chapter 8.

Purpose 4: Leads Management to be "Proactive" versus "Reactive." When making critical decisions, especially facing unexpected obstacles, managing to a Business Plan identifies in advance potential risks and how to mitigate them. The decisions and action steps you take will be more effective if they have already been identified, thought out, and vetted. The poorest decisions arise when a situation occurs unexpectedly, and the management team "guesses" at how best to address the problems or makes decisions in a panic. It is disheartening and unproductive in so many ways to disrupt your business by taking key people and/or employees away from their jobs to try to figure out how to remedy your problems. The more you prepare in advance, the better your decisions will be, and the more likely your success.

"Proactive is Good! Reactive is Bad!"

Purpose 5: Provides sufficient data to diagnose and remove obstacles or open opportunities that block your Company's progress. You cannot make good decisions without having detailed data, financial numbers, marketing and sales projections, technology capabilities, and more. You always need to quickly determine the source of your problems or identify opportunities, then develop and implement the most effective remedies. Data is a critical component of effective decision-making.

Purpose 6: Communicates your Company's Business Model to potential lenders, investors, and stakeholders. Too many entrepreneurs and business owners I've spoken with over the years believe the Business Plan's only purpose is to support financing opportunities. My experience shows that, while it is critically important to have and manage to an effective Business Plan to obtain financing, the other purposes mentioned above relate directly to how the Company is managed, and how it maximizes its performance. **Bankers and investors do not lend or invest funds in a company; they invest in their confidence that the management team will effectively implement the Business Plan.** You cannot depend on external consultants or others to present the Company's performance issues or defend funding applications. The management team ultimately has total responsibility for the Company's performance.

Purpose 7: Inclusion of a Risk and Risk Mitigation Section: Unlike most other consultants of which I am aware, I include in every Business Plan a separate section, which identifies potential risks a company may face, and the steps management will take to mitigate that event should it occur. This allows the management team to understand potential issues more quickly with well-defined action steps. It also provides prospective lenders and investors with more confidence in your management team. See Chapter 9 for more details on Risk and Risk Mitigation.

There are more potential obstacles than most people imagine. These may include everything from losing key employees, new competitors, target markets rejecting your products or services, weather-related disasters, internal or external lawsuits, key employee illness or death, change in federal/state/local regulations, economic recession, and even a global pandemic.

Researching and networking are critical to identifying all potential risks, as well as what is considered out-of-the-box thinking.

~ *IDENTIFYING POTENTIAL RISKS* ~

A good example occurred when I had to create an SEC-required Shareholder Disclosure Agreement for a client company that was seeking an equity investment, and working with the company's attorney to finalize it. The Shareholder Disclosure Agreement included the requirement to identify as many potential risks as possible and how each risk will be mitigated should it occur. I developed a list that was four pages long, with most risks not even thought of by the client company.

I also noted a number of insurance programs that cover items that most small business owners never think about, such as insurance to cover operating expenses if the owner becomes ill or disabled for some period of time, and disability insurance for key employees. The list goes on and on...

Always remember:

"The unexpected may quickly become reality. Be prepared!"

~ THE IMPACT OF NOT HAVING A BUSINESS PLAN! ~

A colleague referred a business owner to me who has had a successful company for 25 years, from which he made a good living. Yet, within the past two years, his profitability became break-even at best, and he didn't know why or what to do. He needed help!

After a 15-minute introductory discussion, I asked him if he had a Business Plan. He said "No, never needed one. I always did things by the seat of my pants and have been successful for 25 years." I then asked if he had a Budget, and he again said "No, never needed one."

Without a Business Plan or a Budget, I told him it is not possible to identify the source of the problems or develop workable solutions. Even worse, without this data, it is not possible to turn an unprofitable product or service into a profitable one. Businesses must make decisions based on data and facts to identify the underlying source of the problems.

The business owner had no idea how bad his situation was. Without any data whatsoever to diagnose or remedy his profitability problems, solutions were impossible, as there was no way to determine which functions were profitable and which were unprofitable, even for a Cash Flow expert. I didn't even have enough information to attempt to re-engineer a Business Plan and Budget. He was destined to continue to struggle financially if major changes to his management processes, his financial statements, his recordkeeping, or his business acumen were not made.

~ A PLAN THAT WORKED WELL! ~

As the Chief Financial and Administrative Officer of the Worldwide Financial Services Department at Bank of Boston Corporation, a $3.5 Billion unit with multiple international businesses, I was tasked with the project to replace the international reporting system for our Los Angeles subsidiary. I had little knowledge of the technology issues and corporate reporting issues at this level, so I developed a plan of action and brought onto my team a number of technology experts from the corporate and International Banking systems departments, from corporate accounting and financial reporting, as well as other key people throughout the corporation. The team and I put together a detailed plan with action steps, responsibilities, action plans, and a well-defined deliverable. Over the course of a few months, we worked as a team to make this happen. I was in the Los Angeles office overseeing the installation of a multiplexer, which, at that time, I had no idea what it did. That made no difference to the project, as the technology people did know and explained it all very clearly.

The project was finally completed, the testing worked, the new financial reports worked, and the system was implemented successfully. When it was all over, I obtained a number of high-end pen and pencil sets and leather-bound calendar books from the Corporate Gifts Department and distributed them to the members of the project team as a thank you. Needless to say, this was much appreciated by the recipients, and long into the future, whenever I needed assistance on a project or had a question or concern, these folks bent over backwards to help me resolve my issues. Treat everyone with respect and it will be returned. Most importantly, having a project plan, like a Business Plan, and following it closely, results in success.

THE BIG PICTURE

CHAPTER 3

MY MAXIMIZING CASH FLOW PROCESS

Once your Business Plan, financial projections, and budget have been prepared, proofread, and implemented, you **MUST** manage to it. When a problem, obstacle, or opportunity appears, it is imperative to follow this directive, as it is the only way you will be able to develop the right solutions. I offer below the critical five steps you must take, in the proper order.

Step 1: Diagnose the Problem(s). Without a diagnosis, there is no way to develop appropriate solution options. Identifying the source of your issues is essential to resolving them. A doctor cannot prescribe remedies if he/she does not know the cause of the illness.

Step 2: Prescribe Remedies. Once you have diagnosed the source of your problems, you can then more effectively develop the appropriate remedies.

Step 3: Develop a Plan to Resolve Problems. Once you identify the remedies, put in writing in your Business Plan exactly what steps you are going to take to implement them.

Step 4: Implement the Plan. Manage the company to your Business Plan. Follow the exact steps highlighted in each section. This is absolute!

Step 5: Continue to Monitor and Modify the Business Plan. Continue to monitor your performance based on the following criteria, and modify your Business Plan when necessary:

- Track your financial performance on an ongoing basis, at least weekly, and even daily, until you have a consistent recurring revenue stream. Always keep monitoring and modifying because change happens.

- Analyze your marketing and sales performance to understand what's working and what's not.

- Continuously review your pricing and costing strategies for each product or service and adjust as necessary. Compare competitor price/cost data as best you can.

- Understand all the other qualitative issues including technology, operations, vendor relationships, staffing, competitors, regulatory changes, supplier status, and more. Make sure the financial results are credible and clear.

Without the necessary data to work with, there is no possible way for any business owner or an outside expert to identify and fix your problems. The business will be in deep trouble. Guessing your next steps could be fatal to your company.

Maximizing Cash Flow means implementing the right processes, making decisions based on data, and taking the action steps necessary to increase your cash inflow, minimizing your expenditures, and monitoring performance. It also means protecting your assets. It is not as easy as it sounds, but if you do it right, you will be positioned for success.

The three phases of my Maximizing Cash Flow Process are presented here:

Phase 1:
Identify issues, problems, opportunities

This phase begins when you experience Cash Crunch and don't know why. You may have revenue coming into the business greater than expenses going out, but not enough to cover all of your expenses, short and long-term goals, purchase of equipment, hire key staff, and more. Your expenses may begin to exceed your incoming revenue, eating away at your cash reserves. Regardless of the situation, your company is financially hurting, and you need to identify the sources of the problems as quickly as possible. My experience is that when this occurs, most managers will try to solve the problem in-house. The result is that the problems tend to get worse until you realize you need professional help. This is the point where you scream out "What do I do?"

Using internal resources to try and solve problems almost always requires key staff to stop their specific jobs to work on them. Without the proper subject knowledge, and shifting human, financial, and time resources away from growing the business, the company will likely continue to deteriorate cash reserves without quickly identifying and solving the problems.

"Cash Crunch is a symptom of deeper management or operational issues."

Phase 2: Develop action plans to create remedies

The "What Do I Do?" question has two solution options, each of which I consider an investment. I use the term "Investment" because regardless of which option is chosen, the company will spend money (i.e., reducing cash reserves). In the first option, if the decision is made to continue using internal resources to solve the problems, the company will still be paying salaries and benefits, providing resources, and incurring lost opportunity costs due to key employees no longer working on their own job requirements, but instead focusing time and energy on solving the problems. The time spent on this special project will likely take far longer than using outside expertise.

The other option is to hire an outside expert, who understands the process and who will likely define the problems and develop the necessary remedies far more quickly and efficiently. This option will also allow your key staff to continue growing the company while an expert resolves the Cash Crunch issues. Outsourcing may be Cash Flow positive in this process. Importantly, outside experts come into the situation without preconceived biases, thus providing you with the most effective responses.

This is when you must perform a cost/benefit analysis, to calculate if the cost of utilizing internal staff to solve the problems outweighs the benefits of hiring an outside expert.

"The management team must decide which option creates the best opportunities for the company"

Phase 3:
Implement and manage to success

Once the agreed-upon option is approved and implemented, and regardless of which option is chosen, it is time to implement the Maximizing Cash Flow Process. You and your company have now diagnosed the problems that are causing the Cash Crunch, and have developed the remedies required to solve them. Those remedies should be put into writing, which requires a rewriting of the applicable sections of the Business Plan, as well as relevant financial projections. Now that Phases 1 and 2 are complete, it's time to put those remedies into action through Phase 3, which is implementation and managing to success. The key steps to Phase 3 are:

- Implement the new Business Plan by managing to the improved and defined action steps

- Continuously monitor performance and modify the Business Plan as necessary

- Grow your company's Cash Flow and internal cash reserves

"Always believe that your cash reserve is not maximized, so keep monitoring and modifying as necessary."

~ NOT MONITORING A SOLID BUSINESS PLAN ~

A business owner was starting a service-based company and hired me to write a Business Plan for him prior to funding his company. We worked together to create an excellent Business Plan with supportable 3-year monthly financial projections and assumptions. His target markets were commercial customers (75%) and residential customers (25%). Once the Business Plan was completed, the owner began operating his business.

Nine months later, he called me in a panic, stating that he was running out of cash and didn't know why. He was in a Cash Crunch. I asked him to immediately email me his financial statements for the first nine months, Actual versus Budget. He did this right away.

After reviewing the financials, it took me less than 10 minutes to identify the source of his problem. His gross revenue was far below budget, whereas almost everything else was close to Budget. I called him back and told him we were going to meet the following morning to discuss exactly what's happening.

When we met, he told me he is following the marketing and sales section of his Business Plan by focusing on marketing 75% to commercial customers, and 25% to residential customers. Yet, his commercial target customers were saying "NO" in every way possible. His primary target market was not buying his service (always a risk). We immediately decided to switch target markets: 75% to residential customers and 25% to commercial customers, as identified in the Risk and Risk Mitigation section. I rewrote the Marketing and Sales section of his Business Plan, as these two markets were decidedly different, revised Year Two and Year Three financial projections, and told him to monitor performance on a daily basis. I told him that if he had monitored his financial performance weekly, he might have discovered this problem after two months instead of nine months.

With his revised Business Plan complete, and clear instructions on how to monitor over the course of the next year, he did exactly as we discussed. We also spoke monthly, so we could check on progress. At the end of the second year, his Year Two gross revenue increased by 92% over Year One, which was in-line with the revised financial projections for gross revenues, as well as expenses.

This is a perfect case study, which proves that the Maximizing Cash Flow Process works when performed correctly. The owner was doing almost everything right:

- *Using the Business Plan as his operating manual*
- *Identifying numerous Risks and Risk Mitigation steps in advance*
- *Actively pursuing his well-defined goals*

His only failure was not monitoring his financial performance until long after damage had been done. By working with me to rewrite the applicable sections of the Business Plan, generate two years of new financial projections, managing to the new action steps for marketing and sales, and monitoring ongoing financial performance, he almost doubled his gross revenue in one year. This was a job well-done.

THE BIG PICTURE

CHAPTER 4

MONITORING CASH FLOW - PURPOSE

My decades-long mantra for Maximizing Cash Flow stems from my involvement and experience working with a variety of organizations, ranging from start-ups to multi-billion dollar businesses to a foreign government banking industry. My skills attained through this experience cover strategic planning, finance, legal, multiple areas of administration, marketing and sales, and virtually anything an organization may experience during its lifetime. My most important reasons and purposes for management teams to Monitor and Maximize Cash Flow are:

- ***Understand the performance of each revenue account and each expense account:*** This is a critical step in Maximizing Cash Flow, as you will more quickly be capable of identifying the sources of obstacles and opportunities. To do this right, I encourage you to set up your financial statements in enough detail to easily calculate product/service profitability, properly categorize and manage all of your expense accounts, and be able to definitively explain financial and company performance to lenders, investors, and your stakeholders. The more detailed your data, the better for you and your company in multiple ways.

- ***Plan timing of cash payments; seasonal fluctuations:*** When preparing your financial projections and annual Budget, make sure you include important cash payments required in the appropriate month. These payments may be for taxes, compensation, new hires, equipment, motor vehicles, facility expansion, etc. Even if the projected payment is expected in month 24 or 36, include it, so you can monitor the build-up of your cash reserve. The more you can pay for these items through consistent recurring revenues, the less you need to borrow, saving you money. As an example, if you are budgeting to hire a key salesperson, make sure projected revenues from sales are increased proportionally beginning in the month following the hiring. If you have a business with seasonal fluctuations, make sure you reduce the revenue (and appropriate expense) projections during the soft time frames and increase them during the heavy time frames, to reflect these conditions.

- ***Predict Cash Flow excess or shortfall:*** When your financial projections are prepared and managed properly, you will be able to easily determine the time frame for when you will experience either a cash excess or shortfall. If you expect to have more cash than expected, you should determine how you are going to utilize it - keep it in cash reserves, invest it, accelerate a purchase or hire, or offer bonuses to key staff. If you expect a shortfall, how will you pay for key expense items - borrow money to cover them or delay an expected purchase or other payable?

- ***Develop more effective pricing:*** Pricing is critical to Maximizing Cash Flow. Better understanding your product/ service costs will allow better pricing decisions to increase recurring revenues. This becomes very important when you have multiple products similar in nature, yet with different pricing strategies. For example, a company may have two very similar products, one which is older and another which is brand new. The company may decide to price the older model at a discount to either sell them off or incentivize the customer to purchase the newer, more expensive model.

- ***Ensure sufficient cash reserves are available:*** You and your management team should project enough cash reserves to have on hand at any time. One option, which I've seen numerous times, is to always have enough cash on hand to cover six months of operating expenses in case something drastic happens. This will be different for each company, so choose what's best for you. If your monitoring shows you have less cash than required, you need to quickly resolve this problem to protect your company to the greatest extent possible.

- ***Serve as support for financing requests:*** Several bankers in my network have told me that when a company applies for a bank loan of any type, they actually review the Cash Flow Statement prior to the Profit and Loss Statement or Balance Sheet. This statement will give them a much better idea of the company's capability to pay the monthly principal and interest payments on the loan/debt while continuing to successfully manage the business. The bankers I work with emphasize that having a solid Business Plan is key.

- ***Develop a plan for investing available cash:*** If all goes well for your company, you will be generating substantial cash reserves as you grow. At some point, you and your management team should determine the best ways to manage this "excess" cash. This may include options such as a "sweep account" at your bank (i.e., an account where funds are automatically managed between a primary cash account and an investment account). You should certainly talk with your banker about this and other alternatives, making sure you still have access to the funds in case of emergency.

Regardless of the size of your company, you should always be monitoring your cash reserves. As stated earlier in the book, when you have sufficient cash to meet all of your goals, you are positioned for success. Without sufficient cash, you will likely struggle. Monitoring Cash Flow is essential to this process.

~ CO-MINGLING PERSONAL AND COMPANY FUNDS ~

During a seminar on Maximizing Cash Flow, one attendee told everyone that she had a difficult situation, where the cash balance in her business account was not sufficient to pay a major operating expense bill due within a few days. She stated that because this expense item must be paid, she wrote a personal check to pay it, expecting that once the cash account built back up, she would reimburse herself. Needless to say, this class discussion became quite animated, with several attendees mentioning what I was stating – that you cannot co-mingle personal and business expenses. The Internal Revenue Service and the Massachusetts Department of Revenue do not approve of this type of activity.

The woman asked everyone what her alternatives were. I immediately told her the way to handle a situation like this was to write a personal check payable to the company, and then deposit the funds in the company's checking account. The company would book her personal check as Owners' Equity, with the checking or appropriate cash account receiving the funds. A company check would then be mailed to the vendor to pay this invoice. This process keeps the financial transactions neat and clean.

I described this type of situation as coming to a fork in the road and trying to figure out in which direction it is best to go; a dilemma common to small business owners everywhere in managing a business. I also mentioned something many small business owners don't know about: "piercing the corporate veil." It is critical that personal and business expenses are kept separate. When you own an incorporated business entity (Limited Liability Company, S Corp., C Corp, or even a Sole Proprietorship when done right), which is sued by a customer, vendor, or others, the liability for damages is limited to the assets of the company. If you use personal assets to pay company invoices, you may expose your personal assets to liability. You do not want your personal house, bank and investment accounts, automobiles, or other assets at risk. Piercing the corporate veil will present serious issues to you.

In this specific case, I told her there was no alternative. She had to account for everything legally and in accordance with generally accepted accounting principles, as well as federal and state laws and regulations. Since the company was required to pay the invoice, she needed to reverse the transaction and make the check payable to the company. I suggested she speak directly to her accountant/bookkeeper to make sure it's all accounted for correctly on the company's books, and that her personal assets are protected. Somewhat shaken, she said she would call her accountant immediately after the seminar.

THE BIG PICTURE

CHAPTER 5

CASH FLOW MONITORING - REQUIREMENTS

There are very specific requirements to effectively Maximize Cash Flow. These steps must be followed closely on a continuous basis and reviewed with your management team and stakeholders - owners, management team, employees, bankers, investors, attorneys, and your financial team. These steps are mentioned throughout this book because they are so important.

The steps are:

- ***Prepare, continuously update, monitor, and manage your company to an effective Business Plan, including supportable financial projections and assumptions.***
  The Business Plan is the most important document you have, as it is the only document that links every aspect of your business - marketing, sales, operations, manufacturing, finance, competitors, risk and risk mitigation, pricing, etc., to make sure every function is in sync. I suggest 3-year monthly financial projections with Year One as your current year Budget.

  The Business Plan is a living document. It must change quickly when circumstances dictate. The more you are prepared for changes, the better decisions you will make.

- ***Prepare, continuously update, and monitor your Cash Flow Statement, including Actual versus Budget results.*** This step is critical to better manage your business, as well as explain results to your bankers, investors, and stakeholders.

- ***Define all assumptions:*** All your financial assumptions must be clearly defined and supportable. This will provide you with solid data on which to make your management decisions, and it should answer questions that might be raised by your bankers, investors, or stakeholders before they even ask them.

- ***Define specific time periods for review:*** Each business has very different time periods and fiscal years to review their financial statements. Some companies should monitor Cash Flow daily, others weekly, and others monthly. There is no specific time frame for each business, as each company is different. For example, if you have a bakery and you have multiple products to sell, daily review may be very important to identify products that are not selling quickly, so you can eliminate those products and invest in making more faster-selling products. I strongly suggest small businesses review their financials based on the type of business and your cash position: either daily or weekly until you have consistent recurring revenues.

- ***Take action steps to overcome obstacles:*** Regardless of how well you manage your business, obstacles or new opportunities will occur. These may be internal, such as losing a key employee, or your product development team completes a new product ready for a new market.

Some may be external, such as a new competitor moves in, new government regulations impact your company, weather disasters, new markets open, a failing competitor is discovered, or a global pandemic which spreads quickly.

You must be prepared in advance to meet any potential obstacle. The better prepared you are for overcoming an obstacle, or taking advantage of an opportunity, the better your decision-making, the better your decisions.

Some obstacles may become opportunities. During the COVID-19 pandemic, hockey games (youth through professional) were cancelled, but one hockey equipment manufacturer (BAUER Hockey, LLC) quickly switched to making facemasks for medical personnel on the front lines. In addition, literally hundreds of distilleries around the country, including Copper Moon Distillery Inc. and Dirty Water Distillery, both in Massachusetts, quickly switched from making alcohol to making hand sanitizer. Thousands of companies quickly switched to remote work, and video-conferencing companies such as Zoom became indispensable to our economy. Always be prepared for the unexpected and turn potential problems into financial and moral benefits.

~ MAINTAIN YOUR FOCUS ON THE COMPANY ~

I facilitated a nationwide conference call with more than a dozen small business owners, most with annual revenues ranging between $250,000 and $3,000,000. The subject was Maximizing Cash Flow as You Scale Your Business. These were all successful companies, the owners wanted to grow faster, but each business had different issues, so there were no common problems.

During the call, one of the business owners told me that she started a technology company a few years earlier, and her annual revenues were now around $500,000. She and her team had spent the past two months negotiating a contract with her city, with $1,000,000 in annual revenues expected. The negotiating team included herself, the Chief Technology Officer, and the Chief Financial Officer. This huge contract would be a financial bonanza to the business, allowing them to grow in other ways with a substantial cash inflow. They took significant time away from their normal duties to seal the deal.

About two weeks before the contract was expected to be signed, the city unexpectedly backed out. As a result, the company lost a $1,000,000 contract with little notice, and they really did not know what to do next. She said they were depressed just thinking about it. On top of all of this, her company was no longer growing as it was before because of these key absences.

She asked me for my thoughts on this situation and any ideas on how they should move forward. One issue I mentioned is that by taking herself and two other senior officers of a small company away from their normal duties for several weeks to focus on landing a large contract, they lost focus on the current business and likely had major lost opportunity costs, and possibly overlooked other internal problems. By focusing on one large deal rather than continuing to generate new contracts with smaller companies, they lost significant potential revenue. I said that this situation is one in which hiring an outside expert to help with the deal may have made more financial and operational sense.

A few weeks after the presentation, I received an email from the now excited owner. After the conference call, she and her team met and discussed everything that happened, both positive and negative. They agreed to refocus on better defining job descriptions, responsibilities, and management processes, as well as develop a new Risk and Risk Mitigation section in their updated Business Plan. She told me they did make major rewrites to the Business Plan, including revised responsibilities, and modified some internal processes, all to make sure another scenario such as this one would be avoided in the future. They also took my advice and made sure all their stakeholders bought into the new Business Plan.

This is a good example of a management team experiencing a business setback and taking action steps to move in a positive direction. They put this loss behind them and were moving forward with new opportunities, and in a much smarter way.

THE BIG PICTURE

CHAPTER 6

CASH FLOW MONITORING - BENEFITS

When you are effectively managing your Cash Flow, and watching it grow, there are numerous benefits that will accrue for your company, as described below.

I urge you to monitor and manage your Cash Flow position on a continuous basis, preferably daily or weekly for at least 36 months. If you don't, you will not be able to easily resolve current and future problems, nor will you be able to take advantage of new opportunities.

The following are benefits of Cash Flow Monitoring:

- ***Ensure timely tax payments:*** All income and non-income taxes - federal, state, local, unemployment insurance, and other governmental taxes - must be paid on time. **This IS your number one priority.** By monitoring your cash position and forecasting your cash outflows for months into the future, you will clearly see when your tax bills are due, and how much expected payment will be required. Compare that to your expected cash position at the time payments are due and you will see if you expect to have sufficient cash on hand, or if there will be a shortfall. This will give you time to make adjustments to improve your cash position, or develop alternative options to pay your tax liability. Your tax bills must be paid on time before any other company bills are paid, including payroll.

- ***Anticipate future financing requirements:*** Your goal is to grow cash reserves with recurring revenues. By effectively monitoring your cash accounts over the course of two to three years, you will be able to anticipate all your expected and unexpected expenses. The more revenues you generate from operations, the less you will require from outside financing, saving you on lower borrowing costs and interest expenses.

- ***Projecting Key Expenses:*** By projecting and anticipating when you will be experiencing cash shortfalls, you will be better prepared on how to identify appropriate financing options to meet your company's needs. The key expense categories that I emphasize are:

    - ***Operational Expenses:*** Managing your Budget means you review each line-item expense as necessary. By monitoring your cash position, you will be able to best determine your ability to meet operating expenses including taxes, payroll, mortgages/leases, utilities, marketing and sales requirements, travel costs, and more. If you know you are going to require additional hires at some point in the future, you need to manage your cash position or anticipated loan/debt borrowing to make sure this can be covered when the time comes. I strongly recommend you do not use credit card debt to pay expenses. It is very expensive and may cause further financial problems.

    - ***Capital expenditures:*** When the purchasing or leasing of new capital equipment is being planned, the company's cash position or borrowing must be projected at the time of acquisition.

- ◦ ***Seasonal fluctuations:*** If you have a seasonal business, it is critical for you to make sure your cash position will be sufficient during the strong months to cover the expenses you will need to pay during your slow months.

- ***Effective Pricing:*** Pricing is a critical component of Cash Flow Monitoring and profitability. You must understand the variety of pricing programs that are applicable to your company and your products or services. Pricing is so important to your success that I recommend you appoint a member of your management team as the Chief Pricing Officer. Monitor not only your own internal costs and structures as it relates to pricing, but also that of your competitors, as well as market conditions and other industry parameters that may impact your pricing or costs. Further key pricing considerations/ strategies are discussed in Chapter 8.

- ***Operational policies:*** Your Company will be best positioned by establishing policies for revenue collections, inventory management, overhead, manufacturing, and other functions. For example, if you fill a warehouse with finished products and you cannot sell them quickly, you effectively have dead money. You've already paid to manufacture or produce the products, but they are sitting in a warehouse not generating revenue. Even if you hire a salesperson to sell the inventory, it is likely that some of the products will be returned because of damages, or they are out of date. This hurts your business substantially. Through implementing appropriate operational policies for inventory supply management in this example, your company can minimize its storage expenses and have a faster turn-around on inventory.

~ A POOR UNDERSTANDING OF PRICE AND COST ANALYSIS ~

A small business owner who had a successful company for over 20 years, was having a Cash Flow problem. I asked him to tell me about his company and the troubles he was having. He told me his problem was a shortfall in revenues, telling me his expenses were right on Budget. After some further discussion, I asked him about his staff. He said his key employee was the chief mechanic, who had been with him for many years and was also a good friend. Although he was a great technician and mechanic, he was very slow. As an example, he said that it took him two hours to tune-up a lawn mower engine when most technicians could complete this job in 30 minutes. As soon as I heard this, I told him why there was a major problem with his Cash Flow, and it wasn't revenues. I said that a Cash Flow problem is almost always a symptom of deeper management or operational issues and was likely not just revenues causing his problems.

I illustrated my thought process with the following example: Assume your labor cost is $30 per hour. To tune-up a lawn mower, it would take 30 minutes, or $15 cost of labor. Add to this another $5 for parts and $5 for overhead, so the all-in cost to tune up the lawn mower was $25. Since the market price for this service was $50, he would make a $25 profit for each tune-up. However, his chief mechanic, because he was slow, would incur a $60 labor cost plus $10 in parts and overhead, for a total of $70. Yet he could not charge a customer more than $50. The company was losing $20 on each lawn mower tune-up his chief mechanic performed. The owner was speechless.

Then I said it gets worse. If four tune-ups can be completed in two hours, and your chief mechanic completes one, then you are missing out on three additional customers. He became even more upset. Then I said it gets even worse. If a customer brings in his lawn mower on Monday morning for a tune-up, you'd likely have to say it will be $50 and will be ready Thursday because of your backlog. If the customer went across the street, your competitor would charge about the same amount, but it would be ready that afternoon. You will lose customers.

The owner was now quite shaken, as he did not have a clue about his cost and price calculations. He asked what he could do to resolve this situation. As one option, I suggested he consider moving the chief mechanic onto the bigger projects so his slow pace would not have such a devastating impact on profitability. I told him he really needed a solid Business Plan and a well-developed Budget and to monitor performance continuously. He was not doing this at all. I also suggested he have his bookkeeper or financial officer keep close tabs on everything related to cost and price and make this a key part of managing the company. This would enable him to understand his financial results more quickly, including pricing and costing. Without these processes in place, he would likely continue to struggle.

YOUR ACTION STEPS

YOUR ACTION STEPS

CHAPTER 7

HOW TO WRITE AN EFFECTIVE BUSINESS PLAN

It is important for anyone starting or operating a business to understand not just **how** to write a Business Plan (which is a book unto itself), but **why** to write one (also a book unto itself). This latter point is presented in Chapter 2. My purpose here is to provide the key steps and processes necessary for you to prepare and develop a Business Plan properly, as this becomes the operating manual for your organization/company and is the most important document in the company. A Business Plan is the only document that links every aspect of your business - business definition, sources of revenue, marketing, sales, products and services, competition, manufacturing, finances, and more - to make sure there are no disconnects.

As previously mentioned, an effective Business Plan is one in which the Company grows and prospers based on managing to it. This means it must be implemented in order for you to achieve success. ***The best Business Plan poorly executed positions you for failure.***

THE OVERALL GUIDELINES TO PREPARING A BUSINESS PLAN

Step 1: Prepare the qualitative portion first, describing the business model (i.e., define your mission statement and how you will make money), the key components of the company including marketing, sales, operations, risk and risk mitigation, technology, manufacturing, and the management team that will lead it to success.

Step 2: Prepare all your quantitative/financial data, budgets, projections, and schedules. All financial data and schedules flow from the qualitative plan. Include in the financial data a description of the type of entity (e.g., partnership, corporation, limited liability company, etc.) and the expected start date/date of incorporation, estimated start-up costs, and other key financial and incorporation data.

Step 3: Prepare a two-page synopsis of the Business Plan, referred to as the Executive Summary. It is always prepared last, but is the first section of the Business Plan. This will include a summary of the business model, target markets, products and services, management team, and a financial overview. **Note that many potential lenders and/or investors will read this section first, so it must be engaging enough to make them want to read more.** If they like it, they will next review the financial statements. If they like the business model as presented, they will read the entire Business Plan. In some cases, a lender and/or investor will only want to see the Executive Summary, so make it a good sales document.

Step 4: Include your financial reports, including the Profit and Loss Statement, Balance Sheet, and Cash Flow Statement in the last section of the Business Plan. Keep all back-up reports, proposals, and other documentation in a supporting binder or file. It is acceptable to include an Appendix in your final Business Plan containing important items and reports for the reader's benefit. For example, if you have a franchise, you should include a copy of the Franchise Agreement in the Appendix to make it a part of the Business Plan.

Keep your complete Business Plan to 25 or fewer pages, not including the financial statements/schedules, and appendices, because:

- The editing process forces you to remove unnecessary "fluff" and better define the vision, mission, and value of your company, while highlighting its most important attributes. This will help improve the document's flow of information to the reader. ***A Business Plan tells your story!***

- With a top-quality Business Plan as your operating manual, you will have far more potential to manage your company to success. As mentioned previously, this will make the management team proactive rather than reactive, making your decisions and action steps much more effective.

- Most potential lenders and investors will not read lengthy documents. At two to three pages maximum for each section, you will keep their attention and interest, while documenting for them how you and your team will succeed. ***Lenders and investors do not put their money into a business; they invest based on their confidence that the management team will successfully implement a well-prepared Business Plan.***

BEGIN THE BUSINESS PLAN DEVELOPMENT PROCESS

Chapters/Sections

You should begin the development process by identifying the specific Business Plan chapters, which best describe the company. Then prepare a blank template (title page) for each section in a

Word program so you can continuously add, edit, and update information, questions, and other relevant information. When you are well into preparing the information, this data can then be edited to form the core of your Business Plan.

A sample chapter/section list in a Business Plan is:

- Executive Summary
- Business Description/Industry
- Products and Services
- Marketing and Sales
- Operations/Manufacturing/Technology
- Competition/Competitive Advantages
- Management Team/Board of Directors/Advisory Board
- Risk and Risk Mitigation
- Financial Analysis
- Financial Statements/Schedules
- Appendices

Every company is different, and these "chapters" should follow your specific requirements. As examples, a technology company may want a separate section on technology issues including intellectual property, or a manufacturer may want a separate chapter on the manufacturing process and inventory management. It's up to you and your management team to set this up to best describe your business to lenders, investors, employees, and all your stakeholders.

In the above list, notice that I included a separate chapter on Risk and Risk Mitigation. Most Business Plan consultants and how-to books I've seen don't include this. Segregating Risk and Risk Mitigation adds proactive value by helping you identify potential risks to the company and how to mitigate them before they become events. This illustrates to potential lenders and investors how thorough you are in managing the company.

Data Dump

I use the term "Data Dump" to describe the process of preparing each section with critical information and data.

For each chapter, include in the Word document all the relevant information about your company that you already know, questions to which you need answers, data you find and how it relates to your business, future questions you will certainly discover in your research, as well as any other information you discover. Your research in developing this process is ongoing and includes, but is not limited to:

- Speaking with advisors
- Networking
- Reviewing online or other data about competitors, industry traits, potential changes to federal or state regulations
- All other methods you use to research your company's requirements

As you continue your research, you will generate new or updated information and data, obtain answers to open questions and develop new questions, and develop new proposals. Update each specific chapter with the appropriate information (e.g., include marketing information in the Marketing and Sales chapter). At this time, just include the information in no specific order. When you have what you believe is sufficient detail, begin to write out each chapter in prose format. Assign specific chapters to the management team member with responsibility and expertise for each of the subjects. Eventually, this will come together as your Business Plan. Do not rush the process; do it methodically and it will work out. On your Risk and Risk Mitigation section, list every potential risk you can identify, and how you will mitigate that risk if it occurs. This list will constantly grow, but it may become your most important section once you are operational.

~ NOT KNOWING A KEY FACTOR COULD BE FATAL TO THE BUSINESS ~

During one of my seminars, an attendee asked a question about a CORI (Criminal Offender Record Information) check for her business. This form includes any state criminal cases in which you are involved; hopefully your criminal record is clean. At the conclusion of the seminar, another attendee approached me and asked what a CORI check was, as she had never heard of it. I explained what it was and how to get one for herself, and then I asked about her business. She said she tutored middle school students online. I immediately told her she absolutely requires one, as parents are very protective of their children and online activities. She was shocked and told me she will immediately request her CORI check that afternoon and include the information in her Business Plan, as well as in her marketing materials.

The Business/The Industry

This first section is the most important one, because it defines the overall business model - how the company will generate revenue and produce profitability. In my experience, defining your business model is the most difficult task because, as the Business Plan comes together, and as the company grows, this will change multiple times. Present it clearly so that any reader will quickly understand the nature of the company. The Industry description must include reasonable enough detail to show whether the industry is young, growing, or mature, with geographic parameters, and how you will make money based on this description.

~ THE DEFINITION OF A BUSINESS MODEL QUICKLY CHANGES ~

In one of my seminars, an attendee stated that she was a personal trainer, and wanted to open her own exercise facility. She had identified a building, was getting quotes for leasehold improvements, workout equipment, hiring staff, insurance, payroll costs, and more. Her concern was the up-front investment to make all of this happen, how much recurring revenue was required to reach break-even or better, and over what timeline. In the ensuing discussion, it was suggested she start her business by becoming a mobile personal trainer, going to clients' homes or offices to perform these services. This would allow her to build her reputation as a high-quality trainer, have minimal expenses to start, and likely become profitable more quickly. At some future time, she could begin researching the opening of her own facility. My comment to the class after this short discussion was every business model will not only change as you develop your Business Plan; it will continue to change as your company grows. The COVID-19 pandemic changed so much, as a significant number of exercise facilities either closed their doors, began doing limited in-club training, online training only, or a combination of the two. My belief is that a Business Plan is a living document. It must change as circumstances dictate.

Each chapter of your Business Plan should use the same process. In some sections you will develop material much more quickly, while other information will take longer. It all depends on your company, the information you have, the information you need, and how you put it all together.

SWOT Analysis

The SWOT Analysis process, introduced in Chapter 2 and described in detail in Chapter 8, is very important in formulating the core story of the company. Each point listed as a Strength, Weakness, Opportunity, and Threat, should be included in the appropriate section of the template, along with questions, issues to research, and more. This is not a one-person job; the categories should be distributed among the management team members with responsibility for each of these items.

WHO SHOULD PREPARE YOUR BUSINESS PLAN?

Now that you understand the overall guidelines and development process of a Business Plan, it is time to decide who will prepare your company's Business Plan. I have been asked this question many times in my career, and my answer has always been the same: it depends on the nature of the company, the industry, the makeup of the management team, the company's financial situation, the time frame, and the internal experience and knowledge of the staff, as well as other factors. Consider the following basic options:

- ***Prepare the Business Plan in-house using your key management team members, employees, and outside advisors:*** Many companies decide to perform this process in-house, headed by the management team. If you are a start-up or a very small company with few employees, ask key advisors or supporters of the business for assistance in preparing the Business Plan. The primary factor is that you involve people who know the business, the products and services, and the target markets better than anyone, so it makes sense. These characteristics are very important to the production of an effective Business Plan, but there are also some negative aspects which must be considered. The management team members may not have the necessary skills, experiences, and tools to do this right, and they will spend significant time away from their own job functions. There will be opportunity costs lost and will take time away from growing the company. Finally, the Business Plan must read as if written by one person, not by a different person writing different chapters.

- ***Hire a professional external consultant:*** Hiring an outside expert to help you develop your Business Plan should be a serious option to consider. In doing so, it is important that any external expert work with the management team in developing and preparing the document, as well as mentoring the key team members on what is included in the Business Plan and why, and also how to implement it and manage to it. Once the Business Plan has been completed, the management team may engage the consultant to help implement it. Any outside expert will come in with no biases, no preconceived thoughts about the company, and will be independent. Internal staff, on the other hand, may have biases or other issues they want to focus on, which may not be the most efficient process.

- ***Use an online Business Plan template:*** I have been asked about this option many times: "Why should I pay someone a few thousand dollars for a Business Plan when I can get a template online for $25?" In my professional opinion and experience, these "templates" are of little value to a serious business owner. Basically, the Business Plan is written out somewhat generically, and you just insert your specific company information and data. Every company is different, and you must present it in a way that is thorough and shows the reader you and your management team have the passion, knowledge, and drive to succeed. This may not be achieved when using a generic template.

~ IMPACTFUL FIRST IMPRESSION ~

I once attended a client's financing presentation to a professional venture capital group. The newly hired Chief Executive Officer basically recited facts rather than provide a detailed discussion of what the company was going to do and how it was going to be done. There was no passion about the business. This presentation lasted no more than 20 minutes and that was the one shot this Chief Executive Officer had with this group. In my opinion, the company was really set up to succeed, but a passionless presentation resulted in failure to obtain financing.

~ KUWAIT ~

In 1993, the Institute of Banking Studies - a government agency of Kuwait - hired me, as their external consultant, to develop and present a five-day seminar to the Kuwaiti banking industry. It was called "Costing of Bank Services".

Dinner at a friend's house. The person to my left was in the seminar. See the picture of a camel on the wall above me.

Brochure Cover

View from my room at the Kuwait International Hotel

BRUCE SHARE

Nameplate supplied by the Institute of Banking Studies

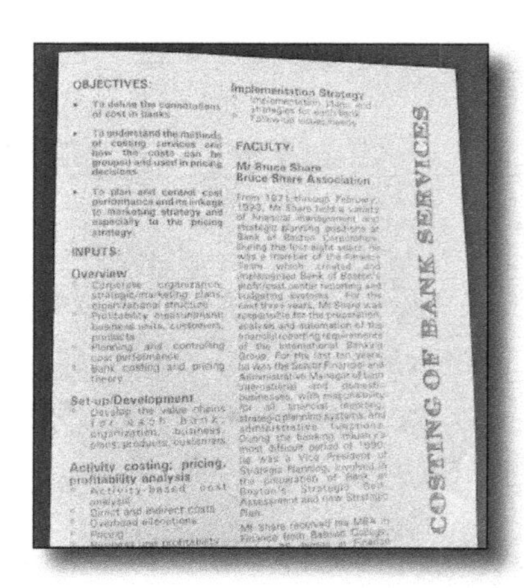

OBJECTIVES:

- To define the connotations of cost in banks.
- To understand the methods of costing services and how the costs can be grouped and used in pricing decisions.
- To plan and control cost performance and its linkage to marketing strategy and especially to the pricing strategy.

INPUTS:

Overview

Set-up/Development

Activity costing; pricing, profitability analysis

Implementation Strategy

FACULTY:

Mr Bruce Share
Bruce Share Association

COSTING OF BANK SERVICES

The agenda included: Profitability Measures, Implementation Strategies, Transfer Pricing, and Product Costing.

YOUR ACTION STEPS

CHAPTER 8

SWOT ANALYSIS

One of the most important tools in preparing the core of your Business Plan, as well as ongoing management of the company, is to create a SWOT (Strengths, Weaknesses, Opportunities, Threats) Analysis. As shown on the next page, SWOT Analysis charts include each of the key areas of marketing and sales, technology, finance, operations, manufacturing, legal, regulatory, and other areas. Once completed, it becomes a key method of understanding how to effectively manage the business on an ongoing basis.

I strongly suggest that the management team develop and complete the SWOT Analysis and implement action steps to best understand and manage the Company. This is true for start-up enterprises, as well as ongoing organizations.

CREATE YOUR SWOT ANALYSIS

Begin the process by meeting with your various managers to assign responsibilities and action plans. Once this is in place, each manager will develop a list of every function under their domain and determine an initial categorization within the four boxes of the SWOT Analysis. You may have to include trusted outside experts if you do not have the internal resources or expertise.

For example, your marketing expert will focus on marketing, sales, products, and services. Each of your experts will go through the same process for their areas, until the full analysis is completed, and all stakeholders agree with each specific category. Once you have completed this SWOT Analysis chart, you now have the core of your Business Plan.

Share Business Growth Strategies, LLC
SWOT ANALYSIS TEMPLATE

INTERNAL SOURCES

STRENGTHS

List all of your Company's Strengths, which may include:

- Resources: People/Financial/Assets
- Technology/Intellectual Property
- Competitive Advantages
- Location/Geographical
- Certifications/Accreditations
- Products: Pricing/Value/Quality
- Market Reputation
- Management Team Depth

WEAKNESSES

List all of your Company's Weaknesses, which may include:

- Limited Resources: People/Financial
- Cash Flow Deficiency
- Lack of Competitive Advantages
- Less than Stellar Reputation
- Poor Market Penetration
- Poor Information Technology Position
- Limited Geographic Distribution
- Ineffective Products or Services

Share Business Growth Strategies, LLC
SWOT ANALYSIS TEMPLATE

EXTERNAL SOURCES

OPPORTUNITIES

List Potential Opportunities for Growth, which may include:

- New Market and Product Development
- Potential Strategic Partnerships for Marketing/Product Development
- Competitor Vulnerabilities
- Information Technology Development
- Changes in Industry: Local/Global
- Economies of Scale for Pricing Benefits
- Attract New Key Personnel

THREATS

List Potential Threats to the Company, which may include:

- Political/Economic: Global/National/Local
- Regulatory Changes
- Lack of Financial Resources/Cash Flow Issues
- Loss of Key People
- Inability to Maintain Technology Capabilities
- Market Demand for Products/Services Declines
- New or Accelerated Competitors Appear
- Weather/Seasonality

Note that "Strengths" and "Weaknesses" are considered *Internal Sources*, which means that you and your team have 100% control over how each issue is categorized. "Opportunities" and "Threats" are considered *External Sources*, as they are impacted by outside forces that are not within your control.

Always keep in the forefront of your thinking that you want to emphasize Strengths, move each Weakness and Opportunity into a Strength, put a positive outlook on Weaknesses, and describe how you will minimize Threats.

INCORPORATE INTO YOUR BUSINESS PLAN

As you prepare each section of your Business Plan, include a discussion of each applicable SWOT Analysis point. Never use negative language when describing items as a Weakness or Threat. As an example, instead of writing "poor market penetration" as a Weakness, present it as "here's how we will improve access into our target markets." Do this with each item in its respective category for each section of the Business Plan.

MANAGE YOUR COMPANY

Once your SWOT Analysis has been completed and incorporated into your Business Plan, here's how to move forward:

Strengths

All items listed in this box on the SWOT Analysis chart represent what your team believes are the true Strengths of your company. Your goal is to make sure these Strengths remain as such. A good example is "Management Team Depth."

You have great people on your management team, including Chief Financial Officer, Chief Technology Officer, and Chief Marketing Officer. You must protect them. What happens if a competitor has a need for a top technology expert and they know you have one they would like to hire? They could make that person a great offer and, if it's accepted, your Management Team Depth is no longer a Strength; it becomes a Weakness. How can you protect these valuable assets from leaving? Possible answers: provide key employees with sufficient compensation, bonus opportunities, equity, annual compensation increases, salary, plus commission and/or extensive employee benefits. Giving them incentives may make their decision to leave for another opportunity much less likely.

Weaknesses

Always present negative issues with a positive outlook. As an example, instead of stating that you lack real competitive advantages, discuss the methods by which you will improve your situation such as improve your pricing strategies, develop more improved products and services, create marketing programs to effectively win customers from your competitors, or hire a high-level salesperson. Be specific in describing these new steps, how you will implement them, and the anticipated results.

Opportunities

Always present your Opportunities with a discussion of why they are such, and what you will do to turn them into Strengths. A good example is that you have a direct competitor who is having financial problems and there is an opportunity for you to take over some of its top customers. Discuss how you will do this, and what you expect as a result. This may include new products and/or services you offer that exceed that competitor's capability, or better pricing on what they already purchase. Make it clear how you will improve your company's performance by gaining new clients from your weakening competitor.

Regarding the example above, better pricing can be an element to help your company gain new clients. ***Pricing is a critical component of Maximizing Cash Flow.*** What is key to your pricing strategy?

- Maximizing profit
- Branding of your company
- Growing market share
- Emphasizing value of your products or services
- Entering a new market
- Introducing new products or services
- Competition and competitive advantage
- Business survival

***"No one pricing strategy fits every company!
No one pricing strategy fits every product or service!"***

Threats

One Threat that really impacts every business in one form or another is weather. What do you do if there is an oncoming storm that could devastate your company with wind and flood damage? Since no one can prevent an oncoming storm from hitting, your contingency plans may include insurance coverage, emergency generators, and outside vendors that can re-supply your company with products quickly. You should always plan for possible contingencies and devise appropriate mitigation plans.

~ SWOT IMPACTS THE ENTIRE COMPANY ~

During a severe recession, Bank of Boston Corporation was required by the Comptroller of the Currency to develop a new Strategic Plan. I was one of three strategic planning officers responsible for facilitating this 6-month project.

We were working with the National Banking Group, the commercial lending department with over $30 Billion in assets across nine strategic business units. The Group Executive and all the division heads, plus key lending officers, participated. As the facilitators, we asked the participants to identify every product they sold, which they posted onto easel pad paper. When they were done, we had at least a dozen pages listing more than 125 different products, from loans and deposits, to mortgages, to mutual fund and shareholder services, cash management, and more. We taped each page to a long wall, gave each division executive five round color stickers and asked them to walk to the wall and put their five stickers next to the most important products they sold. They joked about it until they reached the wall, when they got very serious. No one, including us, had any idea what would happen.

When they finished, they went back to their seats, and we all looked at the pages. There were over 125 products listed, and almost 40 of them had no stickers. After a robust discussion, the Group Executive directed that as of this moment, National Banking Group officers will no longer sell those products with no stickers.

This decision had major ramifications throughout the entire corporation. Businesses, which produced and managed these products, lost their primary sales force, and this required major discussions with these several departments, including the impact on their own financial projections. How were they going to replace these losses? They had to reassess how their products were sold, how they were serviced, and how much in sales would be lost.

This example illustrates that modifying the strengths of one part of a company may impact other business units in a material way. In a matter of hours and without any control over or input into the decisions, its primary sales force quickly turned into a critical weakness. This is proof-positive how every business unit within an organization - large or small - impacts the rest of the company.

~ *THE BRIEFCASE* ~

My briefcase, which made it to Asia, Kuwait, the Bahamas, and around the United States. I still use it today!

Performing analyses can take you many places within a company and even around the world. For example, I had a business trip in 1989, which brought me to China, Hong Kong, and Japan, all in the same trip.

A colleague and I were meeting in Hong Kong and Tokyo to perform a series of interviews, as part of the process of us performing a study defining the information requirements of the overseas units. The China portion was a personal trip for me.

Tiananmen Square, in front of the entrance to the Forbidden City

Achieved my lifelong dream: Here I am, on the Great Wall of China

Jardine House, home of Bank of Boston's Hong Kong Branch Office and Asia Pacific Regional Office

AIU Building, home of Bank of Boston's Tokyo Branch Office

YOUR ACTION STEPS

CHAPTER 9

RISK AND RISK MITIGATION

Risk and Risk Mitigation are critical components to success, not just in a Business Plan, but to company management and stakeholders. Every company or organization, from early stage to mature, no matter how many employees, no matter how well-operated or managed, will encounter periodic obstacles to growth or serious threats to survival, and these will likely occur when least expected. The more proactive you are in defining the potential risks your company may face, and how to mitigate them if they occur, the better your chances for success. Once a risk occurs, it becomes an event which needs to be mitigated.

I strongly recommend including in every Business Plan a separate section for Risk and Risk Mitigation, which identifies every possible risk a company may face, and the steps management will take to mitigate that risk should it occur.

This allows the business owner to understand potential issues and have well-defined action steps identified when events occur and dictate necessary actions more quickly. It will also provide prospective lenders and investors with more confidence in your management team's capabilities to effectively manage unexpected risks.

A sample of potential risks include, but is certainly not limited to:

- Primary target market does not accept the products or services
- New competitor opens in your target market

- Weather disaster
- Company is sued
- Automobile accident in a company car
- Key management team member is injured, leaves, or dies
- Primary source of raw materials disappears
- Loss of a major customer

The list of potential risks should be continuously updated and monitored on a continuous basis.

Risk Mitigation means to understand every potential occurrence which could harm your company, and develop specific action steps to take, should a risk become an event. A sample of potential proactive Risk Mitigation action steps may include:

- Insurance coverage for automobile, disability/liability, key person life insurance, healthcare, coverage of operating expenses, and more. It is imperative that you obtain separate business insurance coverage if your company is home-based, or if you use your personal vehicle for business. Homeowners and personal automobile insurance do not typically cover business accidents that happen in your home or automobile.

- Provide appropriate employee benefits, especially to key staff.

- Research competitors, as well as the economic situations, in your geographic territories.

- Understand and track your financial performance of products and services to quickly identify potential problems.

As a specific example, consider that a key team member resigns to work for a competitor. Losing a key employee not only opens a major void in the performance of the company, but takes away that person's knowledge and experience and provides it to your competitor. It is a serious loss in several ways.

You should develop in advance a compensation package that would make an outside offer less interesting. This may include salary increases, bonus payment opportunities, stock options, or a Board seat. You may want to require key employees to sign a Non-Disclosure Agreement and a Non-Compete Agreement, although the legal status of these agreements typically differs by state. The goal is to make sure the key employee will not want to leave the Company. However, you must be prepared if that person does leave. These steps may include developing "bench strength" by training potential managers for promotion, identifying job search capabilities for a replacement, or reassigning existing staff to cover the responsibilities of the key employee. If this person does leave, you already have action steps ready for implementation based on the Company's situation.

~ SOME RISKS MAY BE TOTALLY UNEXPECTED ~

During one of my Maximizing Cash Flow seminars, a small business owner with about 15 employees raised an issue that surprised him. Unexpectedly, one of his female employees filed a sexual discrimination lawsuit against the Company. This came as an utter shock as he thought everyone was happy and productive. There were no indications that this one employee

was in any way upset, as she never reported this form of discrimination to anyone, including her immediate supervisor. This led to a discussion with the other seminar attendees as well.

The owner was quite upset that this happened in his company, especially with no warning. The company did have an insurance policy that would cover any damages awarded for a variety of issues, and that this policy limited the company's liability to $25,000. Any amount over this total would be paid by the insurance company. He never expected anything like this to occur, and wasn't sure how to deal with it or even how to account for it in his Budget.

I asked him when he paid his premium and in which month. He said it was $1,000 per year, paid every May. I told him that is how he budgets this expense.

I suggested to him that having insurance was certainly an important mitigation device, but it wasn't sufficient. I asked him how he would pay for the $25,000 claim if he had to pay it. He didn't know and hadn't even thought about this. I listed some options such as drawing on his bank line of credit, determining if the company had sufficient funds in its bank accounts to cover the liability, possibly applying for an additional bank loan, or, as an owner, making a capital contribution to the company's account (Owners' Equity). Never co-mingle personal and corporate funds!

I then mentioned some additional issues he must address. First and foremost, this was only one issue. Why did this claim arise? Were there lax internal rules and regulations that failed, or was it human failure to understand what was happening?

Was this employee unaware of the procedures to file a complaint? Did the supervisor have any idea of what this employee was dealing with, and if not, why not?

~ IS A HUMAN RESOURCES MANUAL NECESSARY FOR A START-UP? ~

I was presenting my "How to Write an Effective Business Plan" seminar for the Small Business Development Center at Salem State University, and had about 60 attendees. I asked how many of them thought having a Human Resources Manual was an important resource for entrepreneurs and small business owners. Only one person raised her hand, and she was a human resources professional. We began a discussion on why it is very important for all businesses to have this type of manual. It includes important rules and regulations, as well as policy information on employee dress code, smoking rules, compensation, newly added COVID protocols, and the corporate grievance procedures. In my opinion, having a Human Resources Manual, even when you only have one employee, will pay dividends when you have 10, 20, 50 or more employees. A human resources professional will be able to create one for you, whether within your company or through the use of an outside expert. I recommend you consider this for your company.

"Understanding the big picture is critical to successfully dealing with it."

YOUR ACTION STEPS

CHAPTER 10

OUTSOURCING TO IMPROVE CASH FLOW

Business owners and the management team must understand that the company may improve its Cash position by outsourcing specific functions to independent and unbiased outside experts. These decisions are based on, but not limited to, the following:

- ***Lack of Internal Expertise:*** The company does not have the in-house experience, knowledge, or skills to perform well-defined requirements.

- ***Lack of Desire to Perform Specific Tasks:*** Especially in small companies, key employees may not want to perform certain tasks in order to focus instead on their own specific skills, experience, and job duties.

- ***Small Team with Business Expertise:*** It would be counter-productive and expensive in terms of money and lost opportunity costs to pull key employees away from their specific jobs to perform tasks at which they are not an expert.

- ***Cost/Benefit Analysis:*** Prior to deciding whether or not to outsource specific functions, perform a cost/benefit analysis to determine if the potential engagement is financially feasible to the company.

I highly recommend that the management team members develop a Functional Organization Chart, which is a tool I developed for Maximizing Cash Flow, by outsourcing the performance of specific functions to outside experts.

By following the guidelines for preparing a Functional Organization Chart, you will be able to more quickly and efficiently identify which specific functions should be outsourced and develop the methodology to find the right external experts to meet your company's needs. Outsourcing appropriate functions to outside experts typically results in expedited solutions while your key employees remain focused on their own jobs. You must understand "WHY" a specific function should be outsourced.

My Functional Organization Chart model is presented on the next page. Note that it includes the functions the company must perform within specified departments. It does not include any names of those responsible for the tasks. In some cases, the Chief Executive Officer may be the only employee, a situation where it is likely that outsourcing certain functions is essential to success. In other situations, the company may have only a few key employees, each with a specific skill set. This requires the management team to identify what they need to outsource and what can be performed in-house.

The most effective way to prepare this document is:

- ***First***, identify the specific functions your business performs, segregated by departments such as Finance and Administration, Sales and Marketing, Technology, Operations and Manufacturing, and others. Even if you are a Sole Proprietor, I recommend you create this for your company. This chart is different for every business; therefore, you, your management team, and advisors must develop these departments based on your company's specific needs.

FUNCTIONAL ORGANIZATION CHART

- ***Second***, determine which functions you either do not have the internal staff to perform, the expertise required, or you just do not want to perform within the company.

- ***Third***, identify potential functions to outsource, and search for the appropriate external expertise for each job. Find resources that meet requirements for expertise desired, compatibility with your corporate culture, and cost/benefit analysis between the cost of hiring the consultant versus the likely additional revenue to be generated.

- ***Fourth***, once everything has been completed, only then do you assign individuals by name and include their specific responsibilities. If you are a sole proprietor, you need to include other key people whom you trust to help. This is why a Board of Advisors is recommended for small companies.

~ A TRUE COST OF NOT OUTSOURCING ~

After concluding one of my seminars, a business owner approached me and told me he is a sole proprietor of his business. He said that virtually every day he spends too much time putting out "fires" in various aspects of his business. At the end of each day, he had not made much progress in growing his business because of these "daily fire drills." He was not making as much money as he knew he could and was very frustrated. He said he didn't know what to do.

I showed him this chart and asked him which functions he did not want to perform himself. He immediately responded with

"Finance and Bookkeeping," which is typically the function most small business owners do not want to do themselves. I told him he should hire a part-time bookkeeper to do the books and prepare the financial schedules and reports. He responded by saying this would cost money and he couldn't afford it. I looked him right in the eyes and told him he couldn't afford not to do it. After staring straight ahead for several seconds, the "deer in headlights" look, he broke into a big smile, just realizing that if a bookkeeper performed these functions, it would free him to focus more of his time and energy on sales and marketing, and his revenues would grow. He believed this solved one of his major problems.

I reminded him that even if a bookkeeper prepares the books and creates the financial statements, you, as the owner, must understand them and present them to all stakeholders, including lenders and investors. This is a great example of how outsourcing a specific function to an external expert supports Maximizing Cash Flow.

YOUR ACTION STEPS

CHAPTER 11

BUSINESS PLANNING IN A PANDEMIC

Over the past few years, how many business owners in the United States expected to experience a global pandemic that would forever change the way we live and how our companies survive or die? My answer - not enough! Too many business owners, government officials at the local, state, and federal levels, journalists, and others have basically decried that this pandemic hit so unexpectedly, they were caught unaware and had to make decisions quickly without thorough analysis. Remember my mantra ***"Proactive is Good; Reactive is Bad."*** This is a perfect example of why so many businesses have failed in the past year; making the wrong decisions in a panic without reviewing adequate data can be fatal.

To support this assumption, I performed some research and quickly discovered that in 2016, the National Security Council developed a guidebook[2] with the goal of "coordinating a complex U.S. Government response to a high-consequence emerging disease threat anywhere in the world." This document included various types of infectious disease threats that could emerge, including "Novel Coronavirus." In other words, the U.S. Government, our elected representatives, and many business leaders, should have been aware that a catastrophic event like the COVID-19 pandemic could - and likely would - occur, allowing everyone to plan accordingly.

Evidence Shows Obama Team Left a Pandemic "Game Plan" for Trump Administration, KHN & Politifact Healthcheck, Victoria Knight, May 15, 2020

Has the COVID-19 pandemic impacted your business? Of course it has. Virtually every company in the world has been affected, many in a negative context, others more positive. The key to survival and growth is how you adapt to it, which reverts to our Risk and Risk Mitigation discussion in Chapter 9.

As mentioned at the beginning of this book, the one constant to every business is "***Change Happens***!" How you adapt to it may determine your success or failure. Although there was no prediction that this specific COVID-19 pandemic would start at this time, it was well understood that a new pandemic was almost certainly going to appear in the near future. Even the federal government created a plan of action for WHEN the next pandemic arrives.

The above description is not solely limited to a pandemic. Business owners must plan for as many severe contingencies as possible, to be positioned to quickly change their products and services as is necessary to meet the new circumstances. The more prepared you are for every situation, the better your decision-making will be.

So how do you prepare for the totally unexpected? My answer - do your homework. This includes, but is not limited to, the following action steps:

- Introduce yourself and your business to community and political leaders, including mayors, city councilors, state, and federal legislators. Make them aware of your existence, and how you can help, if necessary.

- Make sure you closely follow crises to see where your company can benefit society - and itself. If a situation arises where the U.S. President invokes the Defense Production Act, requiring companies to switch their manufacturing or services to benefit the national response, you want to be front and center.

~ *POLITICAL CONNECTIONS WORK!* ~

As a Trustee of a Condominium Association, I made a strong connection with our Boston, Massachusetts city councilor. Our complex had one access and exit road onto a well-traveled road in one section of Boston. Next to our driveway was a bus stop, but there were always cars and other vehicles illegally parked there, blocking the view of our owners leaving and drivers speeding down the street. After our second major accident in which an owner's car was totaled, I wrote an email to our city councilor on behalf, and with the approval of, the other Trustees. I didn't know this city councilor, so I wrote as the subject line "Life and Death Public Safety Issue in Our Neighborhood". Within a day, his chief of staff contacted me, and the city councilor and his aide attended our next owners meeting just a few weeks later. After personally viewing the Bus Stop situation, he immediately arranged to have two No Parking Bus Stop signs installed at the front and back of the bus stop and asked the local police to drive past periodically to make sure no illegal parking was occurring. Since that time, there have been no additional accidents, and this city councilor appeared as a guest at several more annual owners meetings.

Another example is I was asked by a colleague if I could help his client get the proper permits to open a retail store in another neighborhood of Boston. He had been unsuccessful for at least a month trying to find the right people. I spoke with the entrepreneur, and he hired me. I called my city councilor, and his top aide immediately connected me to the office of the right department to generate the permits. Within a short period of time, my new client had his permits and opened his store. The client also asked me to connect him with a bookkeeper, an attorney, and a commercial insurance agent, as he wanted to start his store the right way. Remember, every connection may be key to your success.

I also suggest the following action steps:

- Become involved with organizations such as the local or regional Chamber of Commerce. Attend various events, including breakfasts or dinners, networking, and take advantage of the great resources they offer, which your company may need, such as permits, licenses, and real estate locations. Take advantage of these great resources. Meet other business owners who may offer different perspectives, or even provide leads.

- Read! Read! Read! Read appropriate industry magazines, newspapers, business websites, and other informational resources. Keep up-to-date on industry trends, competitors, suppliers, and economic issues. The more you can predict the future, the better your company's performance.

- Join appropriate trade and networking organizations and attend meetings, presentations, marketing and advertising opportunities, appropriate trade shows, and more.

- Participate in or even present webinars or teach classes as appropriate. I have learned a great deal from seminars and classes I've attended and taught, both in person and via Zoom (i.e., video-conferencing), made some important connections, and even improved my own presentations based on suggestions and input from attendees.

~ *SOME REAL-LIFE SEMINAR STORIES* ~

I always begin my seminars by asking each attendee to state their name, hometown, and a brief description of their business. At one of my Zoom seminars on "How to Start Your Own Business and Make It Successful," one participant described his business model as providing services to senior citizens. Another participant immediately offered an idea on other target markets, including handicapped people. Another offered a likely client. One of the participants was deaf and had a sign-language interpreter included in the meeting by phone, and the interpreter stated the correct way to present this market was "persons with disabilities." Others, including myself, offered information for political, legal, and marketing connections. You never know from where critical information will come.

During my "How to Write an Effective Business Plan" seminar for the Small Business Development Center, Northeast Region, I was talking about how to identify and obtain the necessary permits to operate a baked goods company, as an example. I specifically mentioned someone I knew who was baking muffins, cookies, and other baked goods in her kitchen and selling them to her friends and acquaintances. I stated that she did obtain all of the required permits including required permits and certifications. One young man said out loud that he didn't see any necessity to get permits if he was baking chocolate chip cookies in his kitchen and selling them to friends.

Before I could utter a word, another attendee said that he has been in the food industry for over 20 years, and the permit issues are very real. I then asked the questioner how he would be financially impacted if one of his cookies caused another person to have a severe allergic reaction from an ingredient or choke on a chocolate chip. Needless to say, this young man quickly realized the importance of obtaining the necessary permits, and also insurance coverage. I reminded him that if you have a home-based business, typical homeowners insurance will not cover business-related damages.

At another seminar, one attendee stated his business was making barbecue sauces. A second attendee stated he owns a retail store selling spices. A third attendee said he was developing cricket powder. I jokingly suggested that the three of them should talk about putting cricket powder into spices, which then go into a new flavored barbecue sauce. When the seminar ended and I was packing up to leave, I noticed the three of them were sitting together in deep discussion. I don't know if they did create something new, but it shows how you never give up an opportunity to improve your own business, no matter how wild the idea.

~ THE BENEFITS OF SEMINARS ~

My passion for teaching is an important function of Share Business Growth Strategies, LLC. I have been teaching seminars for over 40 years, as well as being a guest lecturer at a number of colleges and universities in the Greater Boston Area. I have encouraged client companies to attend some seminars with me, and I have attended a number of seminars myself just to improve my knowledge and understanding of specific subjects. My seminars and speaking engagements are designed to provide attendees with the knowledge and action steps they need to build and grow their businesses, Maximize Cash Flow, develop and prepare an effective Business Plan, and learn the right questions to ask. There is a saying: "You don't know what you don't know." This may seriously impact your ability to succeed, putting added pressure and stress on management and staff. My goal in this book and in my seminars is to provide you with the necessary information to give you the best opportunity to prosper.

I continue to develop joint seminars with experts in different fields to provide specific expertise in Maximizing Cash Flow by revenue and expense category, and custom-design seminars to meet specific needs. Thanks to Zoom, location is not an issue. Below is a screenshot of the top portion of the Seminars section of my website, www.sharebusinessgrowth.com. There, you can see an extensive list of subjects that have been covered at my seminars.

YOUR ACTION STEPS

CHAPTER 12

HERE'S TO YOUR GROWTH AND PROSPERITY!™

Congratulations for reaching Chapter 12, the last chapter in this book; the one that brings it all together. As the book's title illustrates, *Maximizing Cash Flow is the Path to Prosperity.* Follow the processes set forth in this book, and your organization will be positioned to succeed.

This book differs from others you may find in bookstores, libraries, and online, because it focuses as much on understanding "WHY" processes are important as well as on the "HOW TO." I strongly encourage entrepreneurs, small business owners, and others to understand the "WHY" in order to effectively Maximize Cash Flow.

Let's review the basic concepts of this book:

- ***The Big Picture*** section includes six chapters which define "WHY" you must perform each function and how the results are critical to understanding your organization's financial performance.

    - Important Processes and Definitions
    - Why Prepare an Effective Business Plan?
    - My Maximizing Cash Flow Process
    - Cash Flow Monitoring - Purpose
    - Cash Flow Monitoring - Benefits
    - Cash Flow Monitoring - Requirements

If you are only going through the motions of producing a Business Plan, or the requirements on how to prepare, or proceeding without understanding key definitions, it will likely hurt your business analyses and your ability for Maximizing Cash Flow. You need to know why outsourcing a specific function is more than likely to have a positive impact on Cash Flow, or you may make wrong decisions. Put significant emphasis on understanding all aspects of your company, and you will likely succeed.

- ***Your Action Steps*** section are five chapters with very specific information on "HOW TO" prepare your documents. You and your team - and all stakeholders - must follow these steps to be best positioned for success.

    - How to Write an Effective Business Plan
    - SWOT Analysis
    - Risk and Risk Mitigation
    - Outsourcing to Maximize Cash Flow
    - Business Planning in a Pandemic

Please review each of these chapters periodically with your management team and stakeholders, as "***Change Happens***" and you must be ready to quickly adapt with strong decisions.

Finally, the following are my most important factors in generating your company's growth and prosperity:

- ***Business Plan:*** The most important document is a solid Business Plan, which is the only document that links every aspect of your company to ensure that there are no disconnects in your planning process. Always remember that this is the operating manual for your business, and the major tool in analyzing data and financial performance. Whether you have an ongoing company or are in the start-up phase, make sure you have a current, updated Business Plan with supportable financial assumptions.

- ***Manage to the Business Plan:*** It is imperative that you manage your company to your Business Plan. By this, I mean you closely follow each of the various action steps listed in each section. By doing so, you will more quickly and effectively identify the causes of obstacles that arise and take advantage of developing opportunities. Making decisions based on data and financial analysis will help you generate the best remedies.

- ***Monitor and Modify as Circumstances Dictate:*** Always monitor your company's performance on a timely basis, whether it be daily, weekly, or monthly. I suggest you monitor daily or weekly until you have sufficient, consistent, and ongoing recurring revenues. The Business Plan is a living document; you must make changes to it when circumstances change.

- ***Outsourcing to Improve Cash Flow:*** As your company begins to grow, or when you face obstacles or new opportunities, outsourcing functions in which you and your management team do not have sufficient expertise, or don't want to perform, is very often a Cash Flow positive factor. Spending money to hire outside expertise is well worth it if you don't have to have these functions performed by in-house staff. It will likely save you three key resources: time, money, and people. Critical to this process is understanding

"WHY" you want or need to outsource a specific function, to make sure it's done right.

- ***Sufficient Working Capital (cash reserves and liquidity) is Vital to Your Company:*** In my research and experience, lack of Working Capital will likely be fatal to your company's survival. With the cash necessary to meet your goals, you can do everything you need to do to succeed. Lack of sufficient capital will force you to make decisions about which invoices to pay and which to delay, hold off on purchasing key assets or hiring staff, and so much more. One of my long-time colleagues, an insurance and financial services guru, told me his sales pitch is simple: "What keeps you awake at night?" This works just as well with your company.

- ***Know Your Target Markets:*** This factor is critical to your company's capability to sell your products and services. The more you can focus in on your primary target market, up to and including identifying potential customers by name, the more successful you will likely be.

- ***Management Team and Stakeholder Buy-in:*** It is essential that all stakeholders - management team, employees, external advisors, lenders, and investors - buy into your Business Plan, the strategies you set forth, and the financial projections to make it work well.

- ***Board of Directors or Board of Advisors:*** These are key team players who will provide the management team with expertise across a broad section of categories. I suggest monthly meetings to make sure they are all up-to-date on the company's performance, issues, financial situation, and more.

MY FINAL THOUGHTS

For five decades, I have been passionate about helping organizations succeed, whether they be start-up or successful small companies, multi-billion dollar business units in a large corporation, non-profits, or even the Kuwaiti banking industry. While I have developed, written, consulted, and helped implement numerous Business Plans over the years, I have truly loved teaching, which I have done continuously for numerous organizations, as well as schools and professional organizations. The COVID-19 pandemic gave me the impetus to put my thoughts into a book for professionals young and old - as well as those in-between. This book contains my career-long experiences with real stories to illustrate important points.

The management team is ultimately responsible for the success or failure of a company. No one can legitimately pass blame to an employee, an outside advisor, consultant, attorney, accountant, or anyone else. Your lenders and investors will look to you and your team to explain performance, support new strategies, and lead the company to success. This book was written to provide you and your team with the basic information necessary to understand both "WHY" and "HOW TO" in building and growing a company.

Now it's time for you to put this information and knowledge to work. I wish you well in building your company. I end by offering you my favorite toast:

Here's to Your Growth and Prosperity!™

BIOGRAPHY

Bruce J. Share has been the Managing Director and Cash Flow Solutionist™ at Share Business Growth Strategies, LLC since 1993. He is an expert in Maximizing Cash Flow using Business Plans, Budgets, and Monitoring as his primary tools, as well as preparing, producing, and implementing effective Business Plans. Bruce has a broad and growing network of professionals in virtually all business categories which, when appropriate, he will refer to his clients with specific needs. He also has a number of strategic relationships with companies, which provide bank and non-bank financing options, as well as expense and tax planning/savings opportunities.

Bruce's consulting practice focuses on entrepreneurs, small and early-stage businesses, non-profits, and ongoing businesses with Cash Flow or growth issues. His first client was the Government of Kuwait, which hired Bruce to develop and present a five-day seminar to the Kuwaiti banking industry to help them recover after liberation from the Iraqi occupation.

Prior to founding his consulting practice, Bruce spent 22 years at Bank of Boston Corporation, where he was a senior level financial and administrative manager for multi-billion dollar domestic and international strategic business units. During the real estate recession of 1989-1991, he was one of three Strategic Planning Officers who successfully developed a new Corporate Strategic Plan for Bank of Boston Corporation, which was approved by the Board of Directors.

Bruce continues to present his small business seminars on a variety of subjects for the SBDC Northeast Region, The Enterprise Center at Salem State University, and independently.

Since 2018, he has taught eight-session custom designed seminars titled "How to Start Your Own Business and Make It Successful" for the Adult Education Program at Keefe Technical School in Framingham, Massachusetts. He has been a guest speaker to entrepreneurship and finance classes at Babson College, Boston College, Bentley University, Dean College, Northern Essex Community College, and Fisher College. Bruce facilitated a nationwide conference call on "Maximizing Cash Flow as You Scale Your Business" to graduates of Interise's Streetwise MBA™ Program, and he taught International Management to juniors at Fisher College.

Bruce has provided pro bono services to a number of non-profit organizations, including the Defeat Diabetes Foundation of Madeira Beach, Florida (six years as Secretary, as well as Secretary of its Board of Directors and the Finance Committee); and Coastal Food Shed of New Bedford, Massachusetts, where he provided a complete review and analysis of the organization's Strategic Plan.

For eight years, Bruce was on the Board of Trustees of his condominium association in Boston, where he was mostly responsible for the financial reporting and budgeting processes, monitoring and projecting the Reserve Account performance, and managing a six-figure road replacement project.

Bruce has a Bachelor of Science degree in Finance from Long Island University, plus a Master of Business Administration and a Certificate in Advanced Management from Babson College. He has been a Business Plan evaluator in Babson College's Graduate and Undergraduate Business Plan competition for over 20 years and has been a Coach in Babson College's Coaching for Leadership and Teamwork Program.

CPSIA information can be obtained
at www.ICGtesting.com
Printed in the USA
BVHW090825111021
618669BV00017B/532